To You We Give All Praise

Music for the Prayers of Saint Francis of Assisi

Words by St. Francis of Assisi
Music by Joe Higginbotham, OFS

Saints Francis and Clare Press

Introduction

Sr. Agnes Marie Regan, OSF

St. Francis of Assisi was permeated with Sacred Scripture and a deeply contemplative spirit. He lived and breathed the word of God. Thus, it's no surprise that the prayers he composed for himself and his followers reflect his profound nearness to God. In our own day, when we use the very words of St. Francis to pray, they flow from our lips as naturally as day follows night.

This joyful book is a musical gift, making the prayers of St. Francis easily singable and, as such, easily memorized—until they are as natural as the Our Father and the Hail Mary. When you find yourself walking around the house humming these melodies or gently, quietly, repeating these words in your heart, you will know that the deep spirit of praise and adoration of St. Francis has seeped into the very core of your heart. These words will become not only the prayers of a profoundly lovable saint who lived 800 years ago; they will become the deep sentiments of your being, fully in love with Jesus.

A CD recording of this music is available from the publisher.

© 2012 by Joe Higginbotham
The text of the songs and psalms of St. Francis are from *Francis of Assisi, Early Documents: Volume One, The Saint*, edited by Regis J. Armstrong, J. A. Wayne Hellmann and William J. Short. New City Press, 202 Cardinal Rd., Hyde Park, New York, 1999. Used by permission of the copyright holder, Franciscan Institute of St. Bonaventure University, St. Bonaventure, NY.
All rights reserved. No part of this book may be copied or transmitted in any form without permission in writing from the publisher.
ISBN: 978-0-9789684-0-3
Engraving and layout by Bruce Munson, Munson Music Services.
Copy editing by Tom Noe.
Cover photo: Melisa Schlunt. Used with permission. Sculptor: Fiorenzo Baccio.
Publisher: Saints Francis and Clare Press, PO box 681, Mishawaka, IN 46546.
Phone: 574-514-0395. E-mail: joe@saintsfrancisandclarepress.com
Printed in the USA.

CONTENTS

- 2   The Prayer Before the Crucifix
- 4   We Adore You
- 6   For He Is Our Power and Strength
- 8   Let Us Speak Well
- 12   Fear and Honor
- 15   We Thank You for Yourself
- 19   The Praises of God
- 22   Canticle of the Creatures
- 24   Listen
- 32   The Humility of God
- 34   The Fire of the Holy Spirit
- 36   May the Lord Bless You
- 37   O, Our Father Most Holy
- 51   Hail, Queen Wisdom
- 54   Hail, Our Lady

The Office of the Passion

- 56   Our Father
- 57   Praises To Be Said at All the Hours
- 61   All-Powerful, Most Holy (a)
- 62   All-Powerful, Most Holy (b)
- 65   Holy Virgin Mary
- 71   Psalm 1
- 72   Psalm 2
- 73   Psalm 3
- 74   Psalm 4
- 75   Psalm 5
- 76   Psalm 6
- 78   Psalm 7
- 79   Psalm 8
- 80   Psalm 9

81	Psalm 10
82	Psalm 11
83	Psalm 12
84	Psalm 13
85	Psalm 14
86	Psalm 15
65	Holy Virgin Mary
88	Blessing – Dismissal (a)
88	Blessing – Dismissal (b)
90	The Prayer of Saint Francis

The Prayer Before the Crucifix

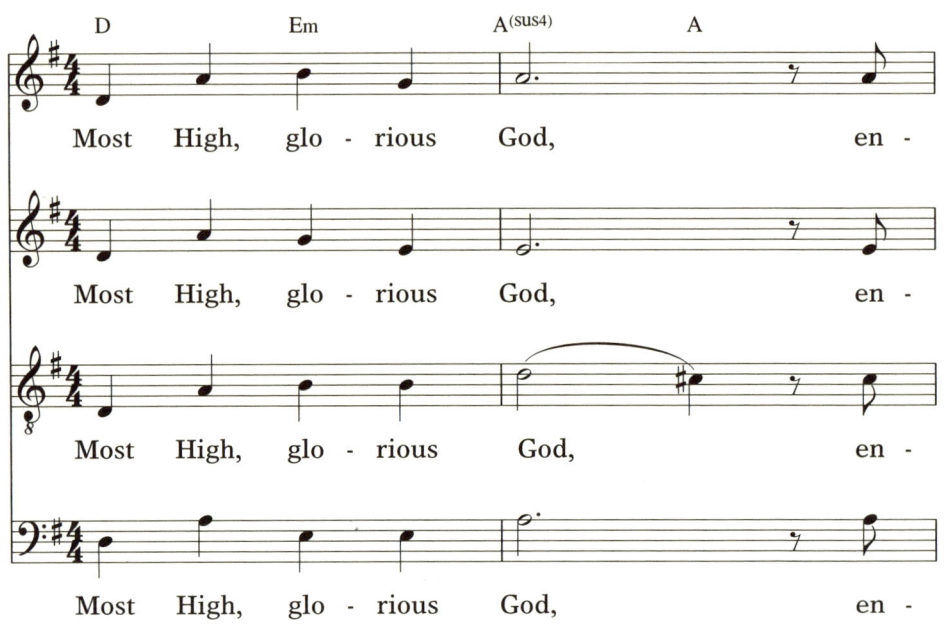

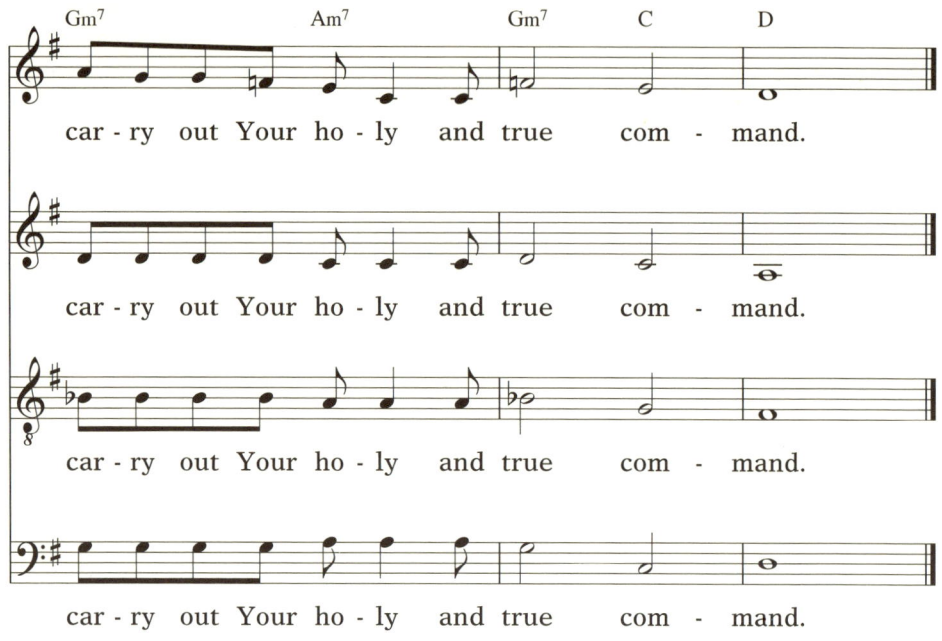

Text: Saint Francis of Assisi, 1182-1226, trans. © 1999 Franciscan Institute of St. Bonaventure University
Music: Joe Higginbotham, b.1953, © 2012 Joe Higginbotham

We Adore You

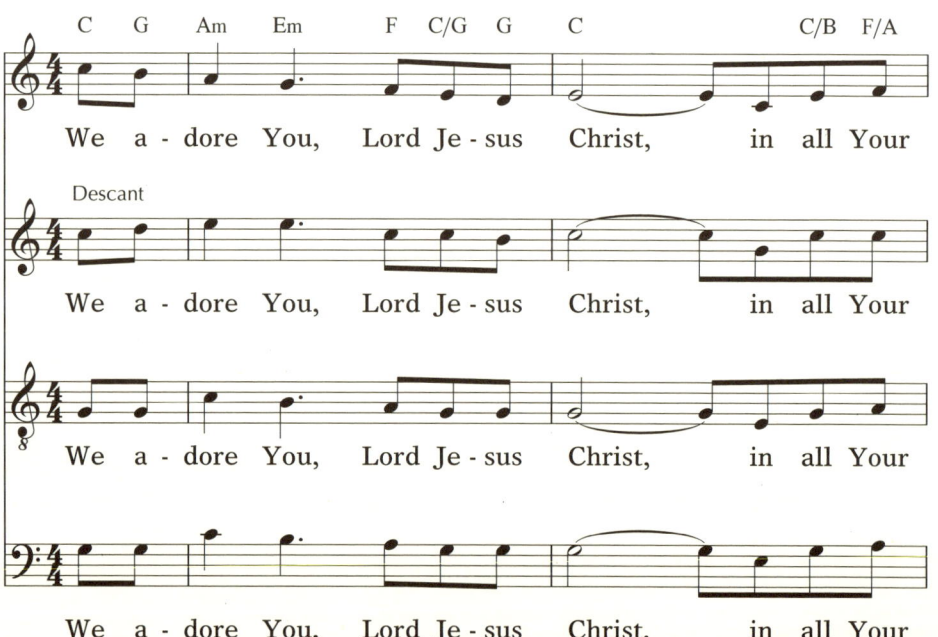

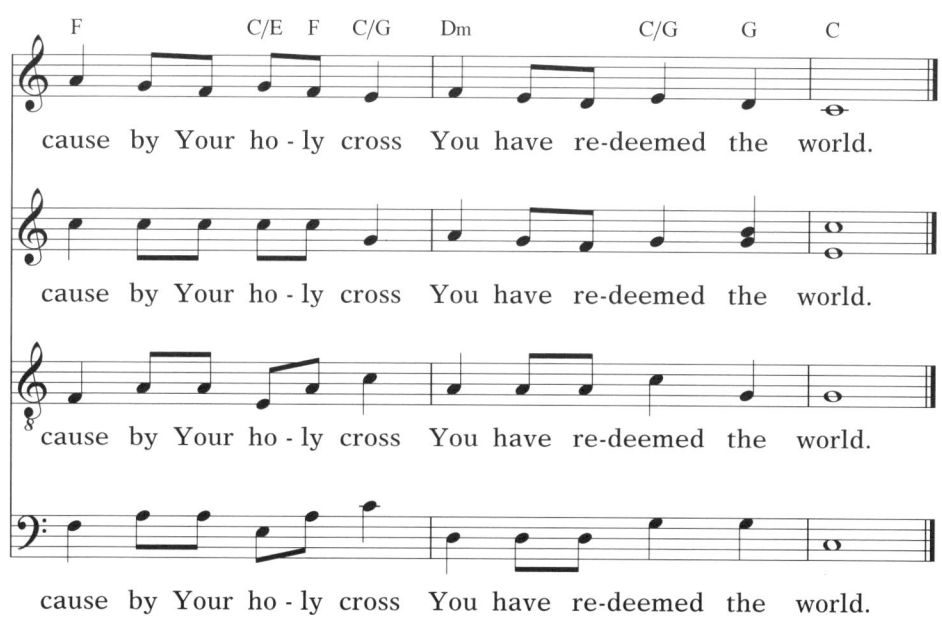

Text: Saint Francis of Assisi, 1182-1226, trans. © 1999 Franciscan Institute of St. Bonaventure University
Music: Joe Higginbotham, b.1953, © 2012 Joe Higginbotham

For He Is Our Power and Strength

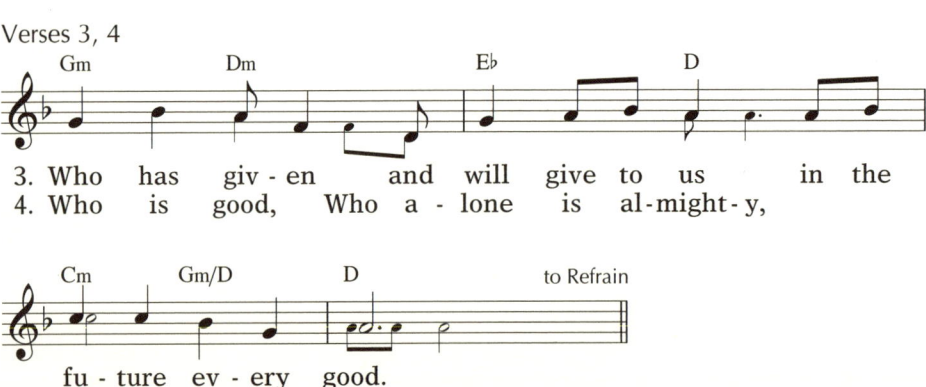

Text: Saint Francis of Assisi, 1182-1226, trans. © 1999 Franciscan Institute of St. Bonaventure University
Music: Joe Higginbotham, b.1953, © 2012 Joe Higginbotham

Let Us Speak Well

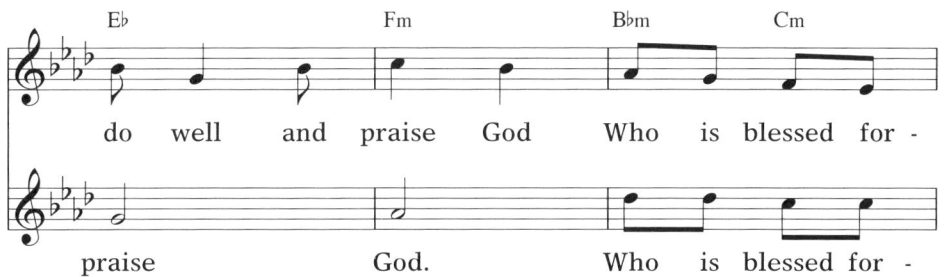
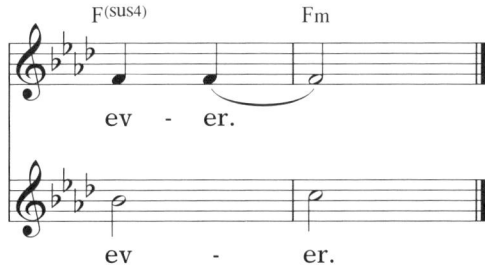

Text: Saint Francis of Assisi, 1182-1226, trans. © 1999 Franciscan Institute of St. Bonaventure University
Music: Joe Higginbotham, b.1953, © 2012 Joe Higginbotham

Fear and Honor

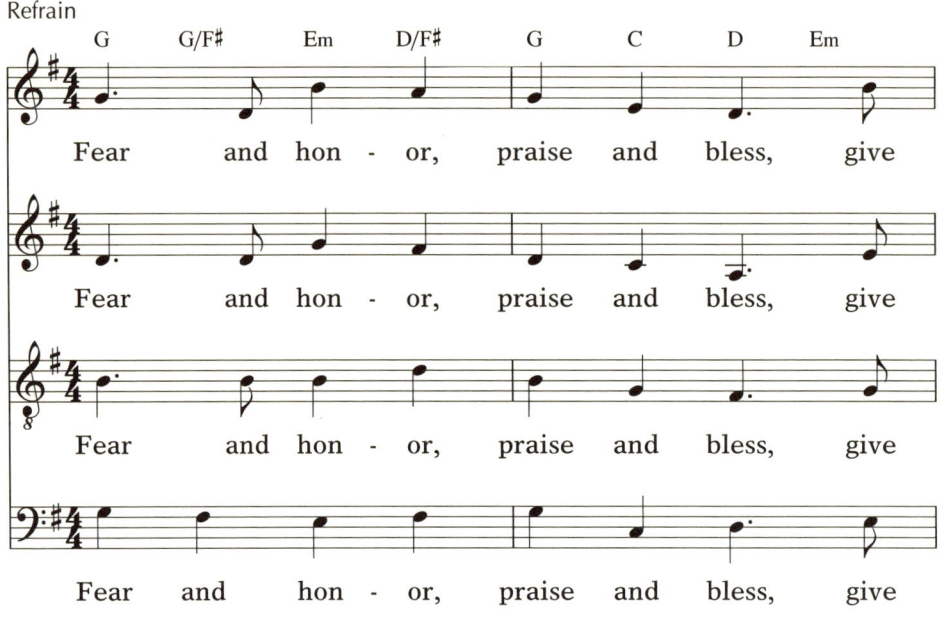
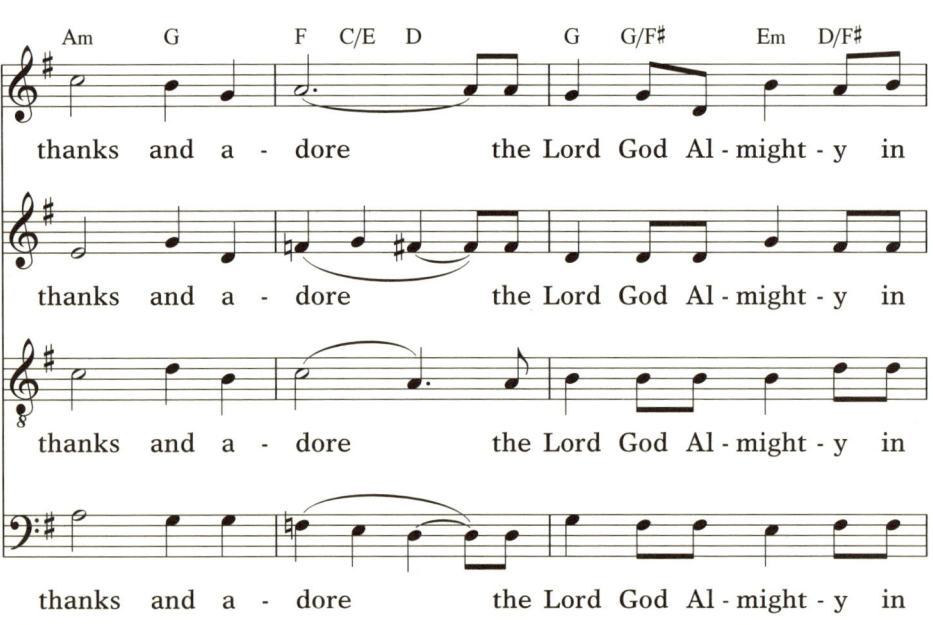

15

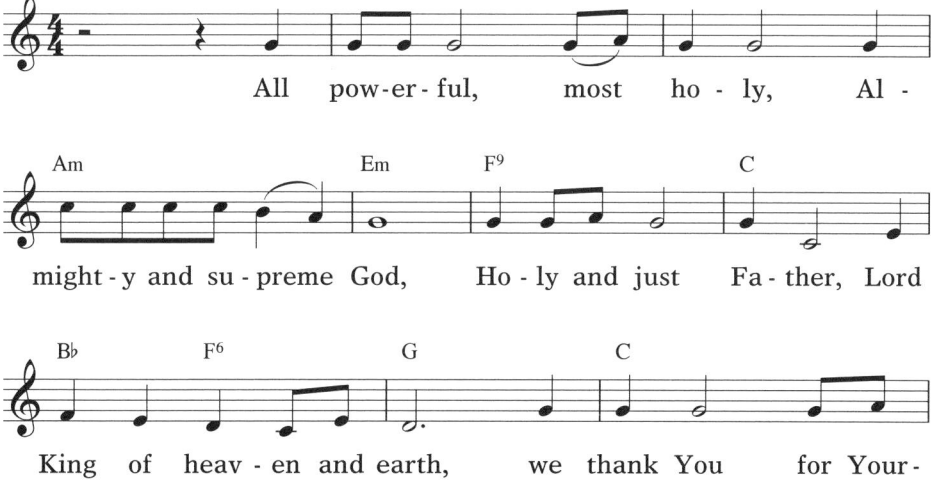

We Thank You for Yourself

Text: Saint Francis of Assisi, 1182-1226, trans. © 1999 Franciscan Institute of St. Bonaventure University
Music: Joe Higginbotham, b.1953, © 2012 Joe Higginbotham

Text: Saint Francis of Assisi, 1182-1226, trans. © 1999 Franciscan Institute of St. Bonaventure University
Music: Joe Higginbotham, b.1953, © 2012 Joe Higginbotham

Text: Saint Francis of Assisi, 1182-1226, trans. © 1999 Franciscan Institute of St. Bonaventure University
Music: Joe Higginbotham, b.1953, © 2012 Joe Higginbotham

Canticle of the Creatures

Most High, Al-might-y Fa-ther, We
Praised be our great Cre-a-tor, Who
O Spir-it, now we praise You, We
Praised be our gen-tle Sav-ior And

hon-or You to-day. For You a-lone are
gives us sis-ter moon. She leads us through the
thank You for Your fire. Through whom You light the
Sis-ter ho-ly death, From whom there's no es-

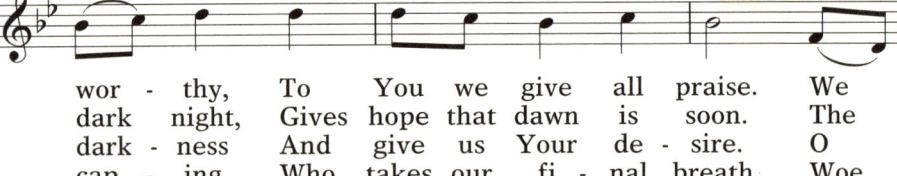

wor-thy, To You we give all praise. We
dark night, Gives hope that dawn is soon. The
dark-ness And give us Your de-sire. O
cap-ing, Who takes our fi-nal breath. Woe

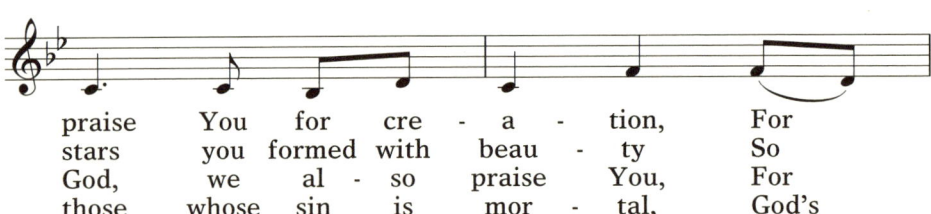

praise You for cre-a-tion, For
stars you formed with beau-ty So
God, we al-so praise You, For
those whose sin is mor-tal, God's

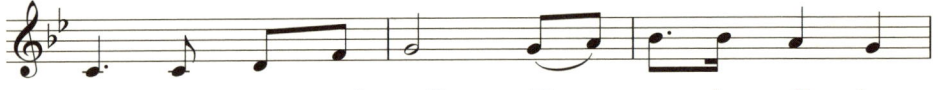

crea-tures great and small, The sun in all its
pre-cious to be-hold. So clear, so good, so
earth from which You send All fruit and grain that
grace they do dis-dain. Thus nev-er will they

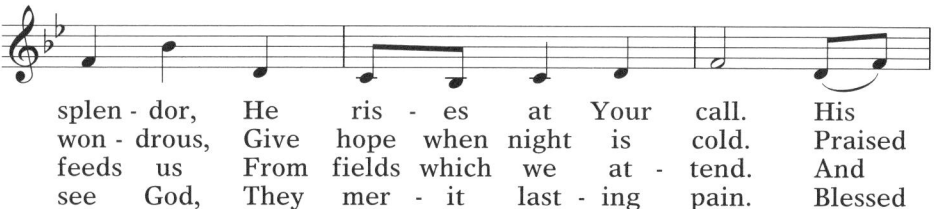

splen - dor, He ris - es at Your call. His
won - drous, Give hope when night is cold. Praised
feeds us From fields which we at - tend. And
see God, They mer - it last - ing pain. Blessed

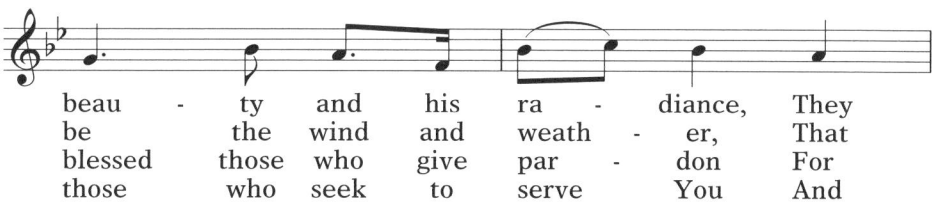

beau - ty and his ra - diance, They
be the wind and weath - er, That
blessed those who give par - don For
those who seek to serve You And

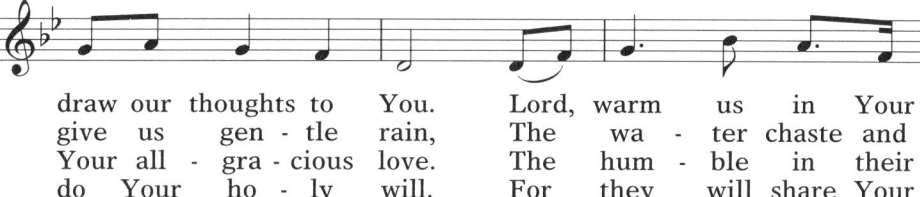

draw our thoughts to You. Lord, warm us in Your
give us gen - tle rain, The wa - ter chaste and
Your all - gra - cious love. The hum - ble in their
do Your ho - ly will. For they will share Your

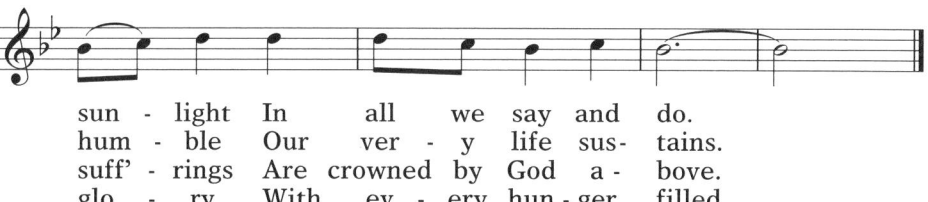

sun - light In all we say and do.
hum - ble Our ver - y life sus - tains.
suff' - rings Are crowned by God a - bove.
glo - ry With ev - ery hun - ger filled.

Text: Based on the Canticle of the Creatures by Saint Francis of Assisi, 1182-1226 © 2012 Joe Higginbotham
Music: THAXTED, 76 76 76D; Gustav T. Holst, 1874-1934

Listen

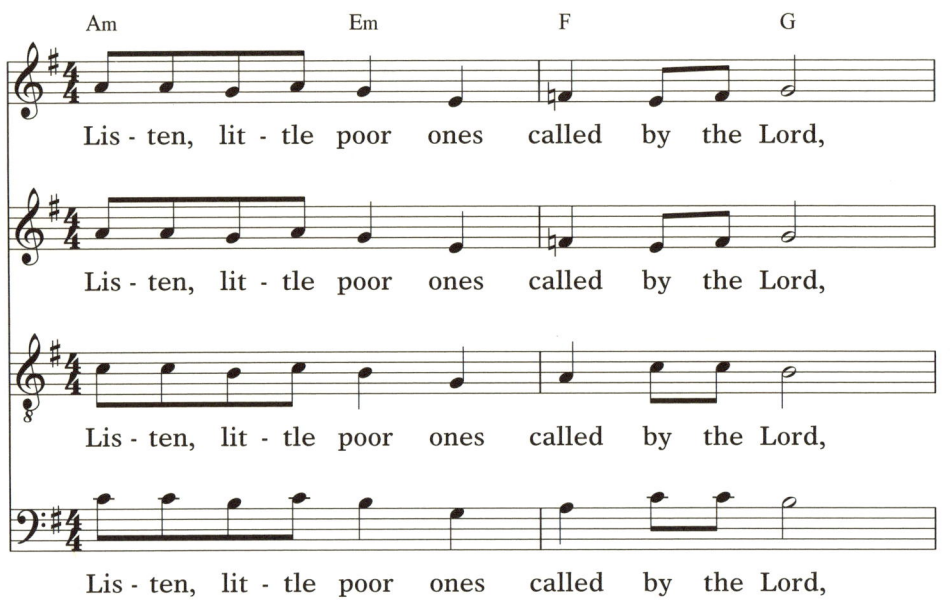

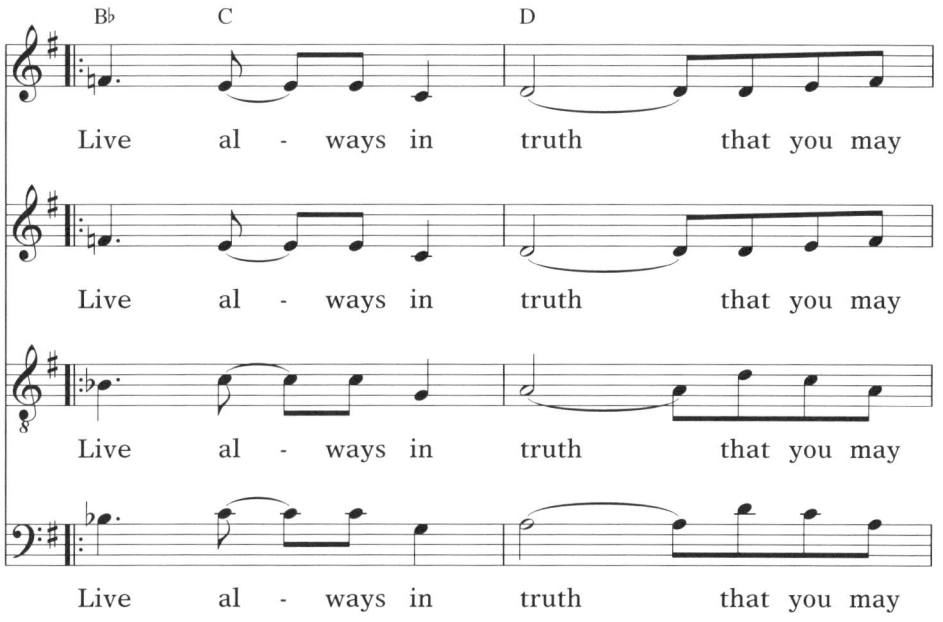
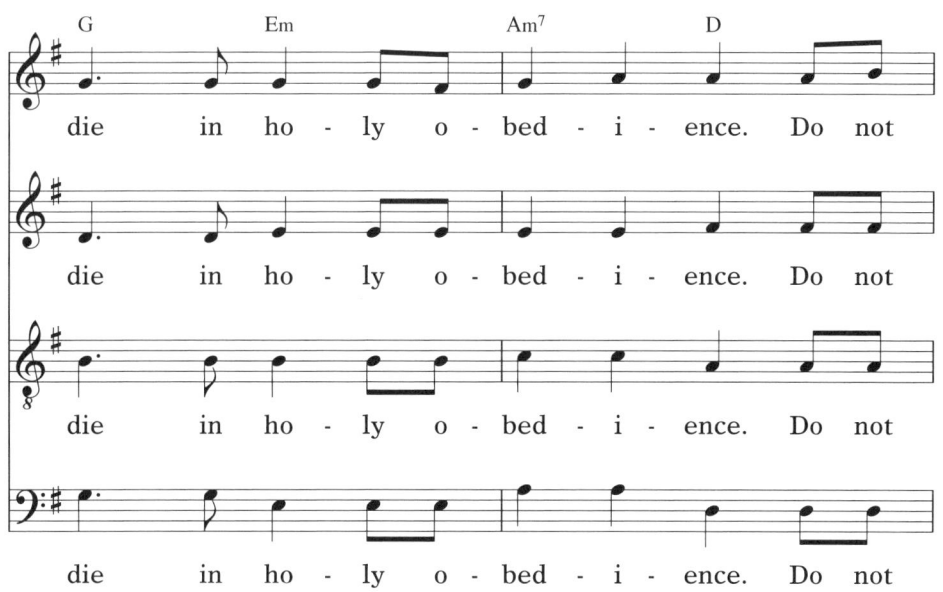

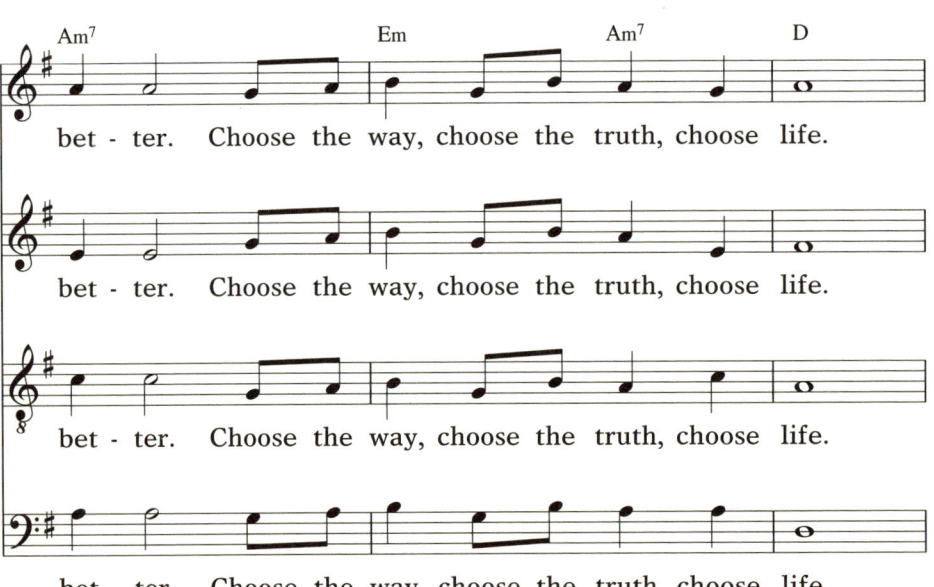

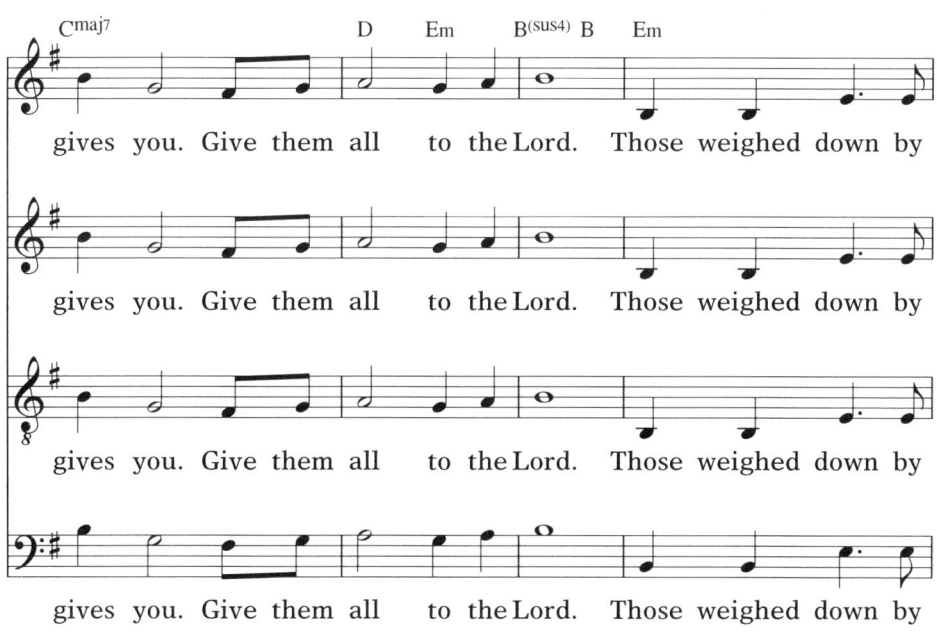

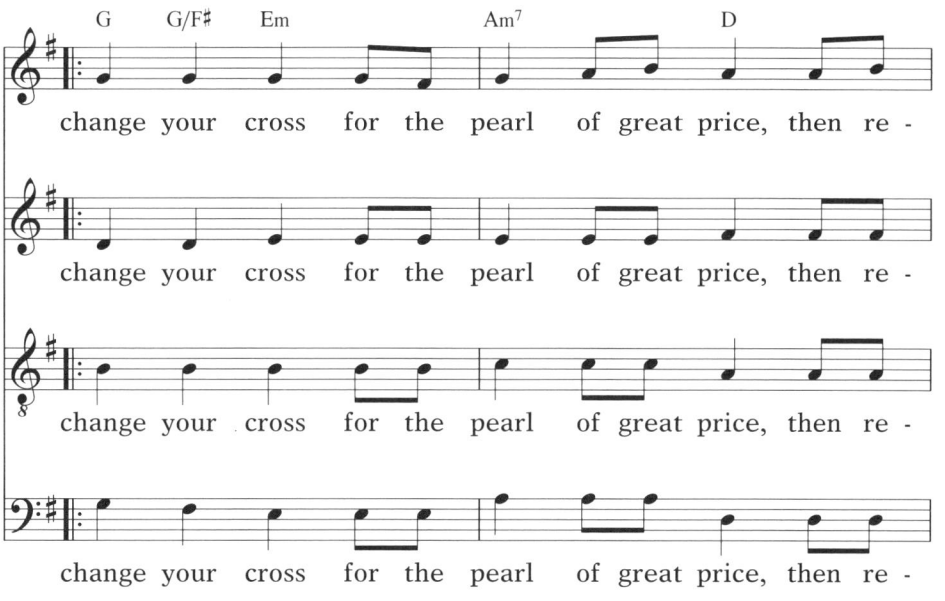
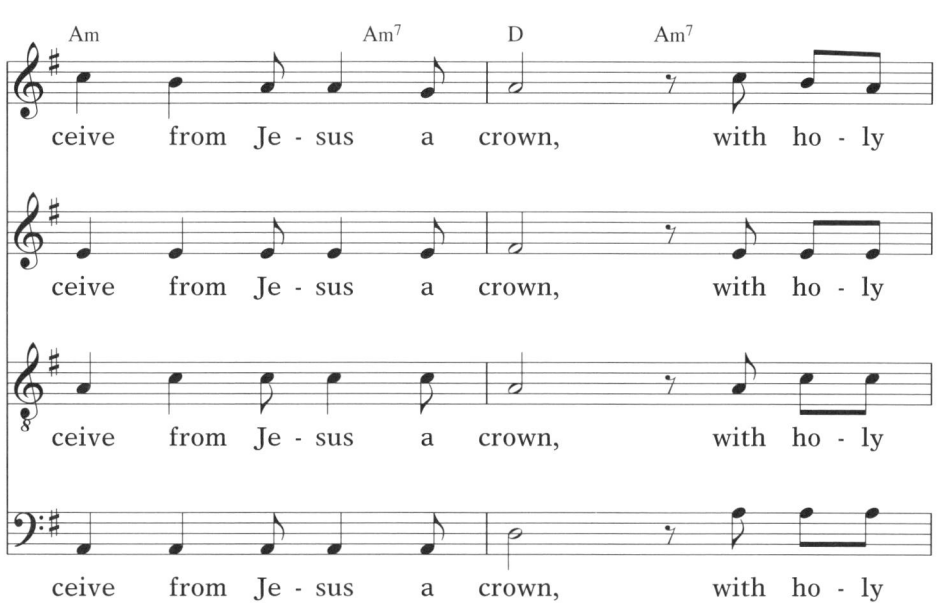

30

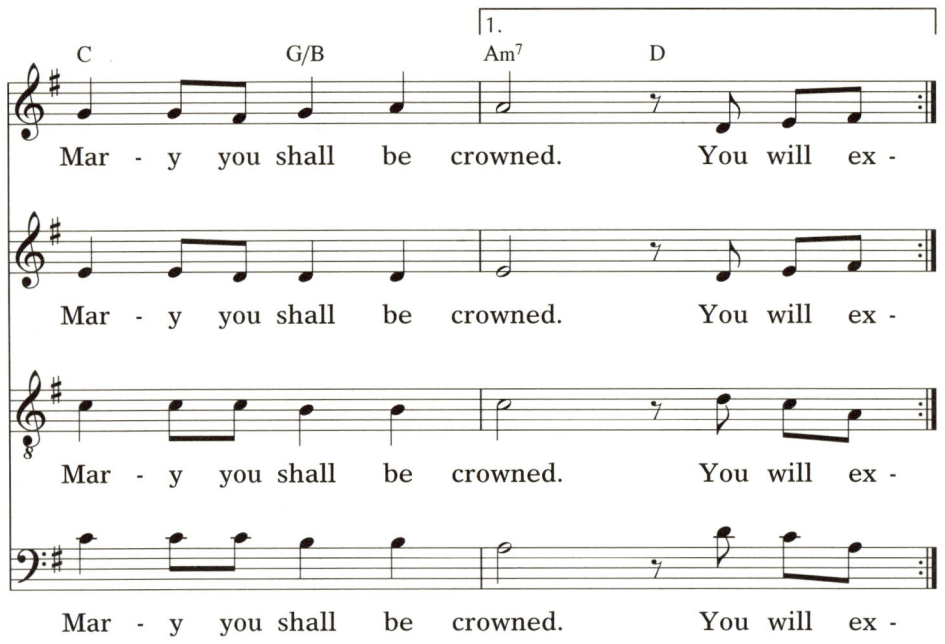

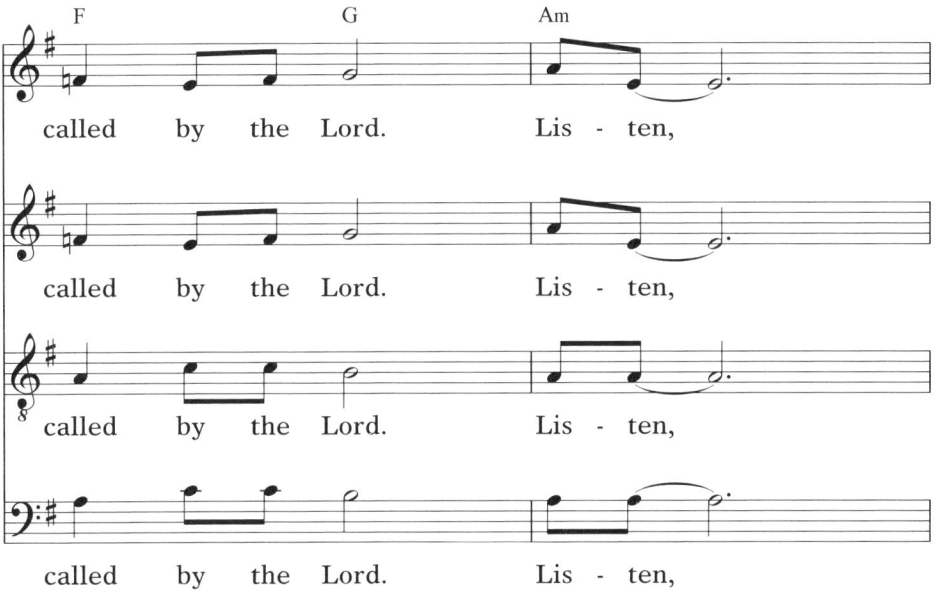

Text: Saint Francis of Assisi, 1182-1226, trans. © 1999 Franciscan Institute of St. Bonaventure University
Music: Joe Higginbotham, b.1953, © 2012 Joe Higginbotham

The Humility of God

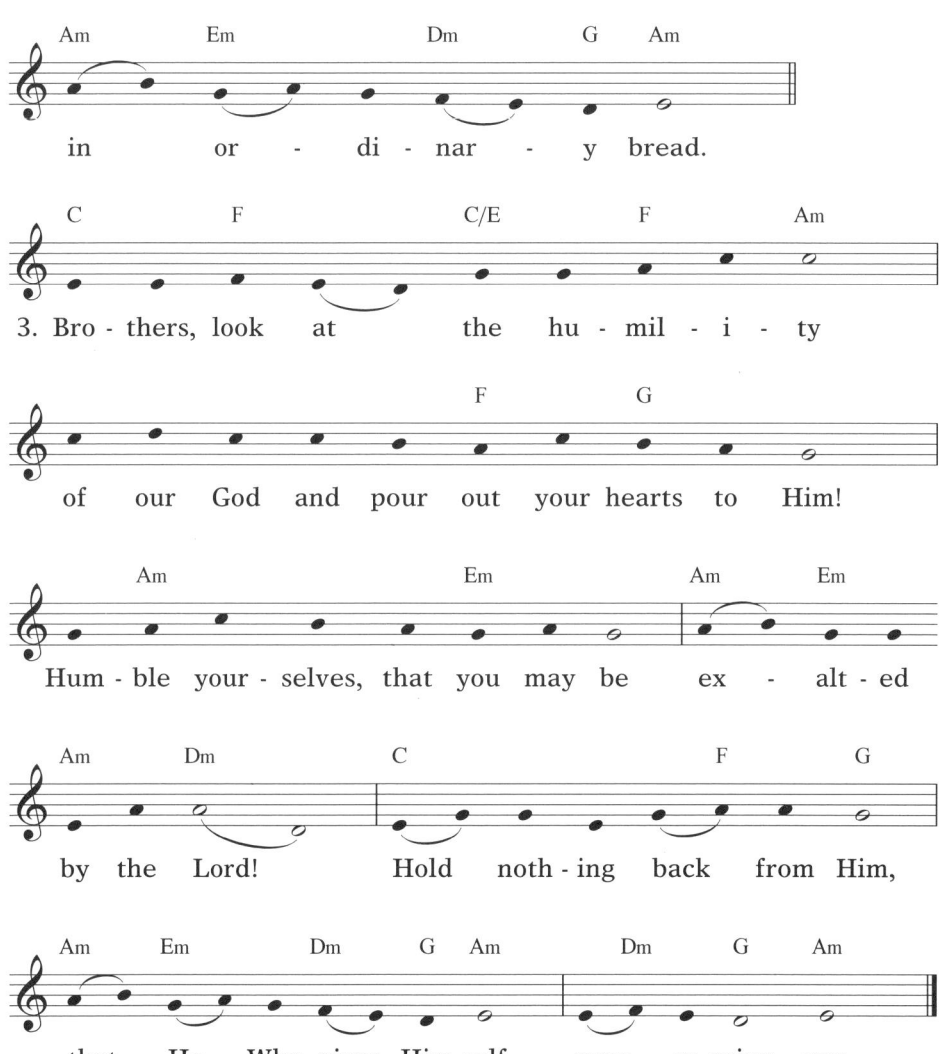

The Fire of the Holy Spirit

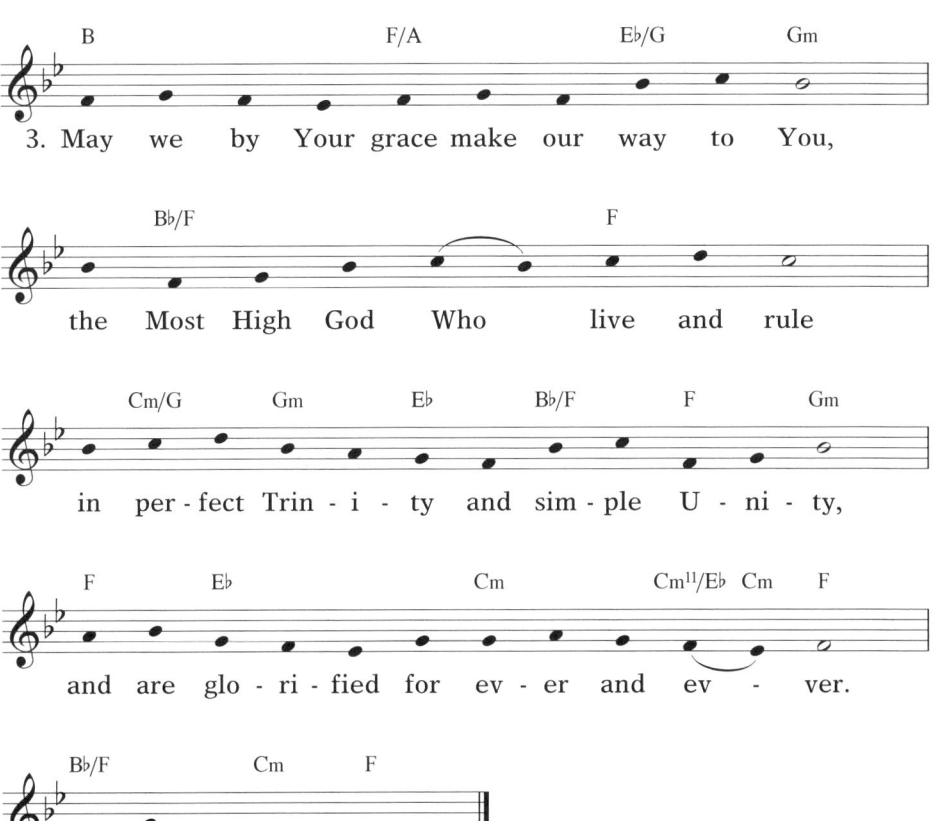

Text: Saint Francis of Assisi, 1182-1226, trans. © 1999 Franciscan Institute of St. Bonaventure University
Music: JESU DULCIS MEMORIA, Chant; adapted by Joe Higginbotham, b.1953, © 2012 Joe Higginbotham

May the Lord Bless You

May the Lord bless you and keep you.

May He show His face to you and be merciful to

you. May He turn His countenance to you,

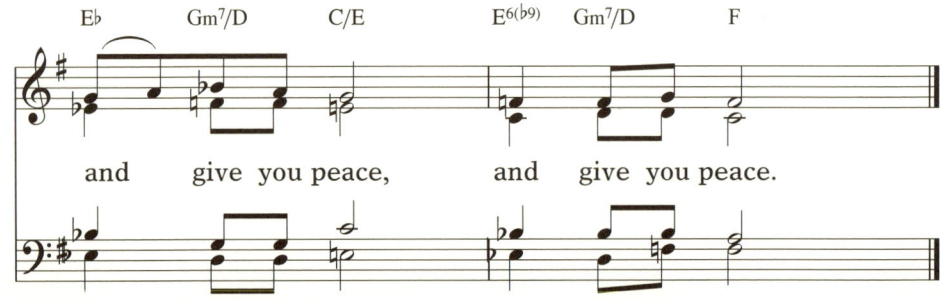
and give you peace, and give you peace.

Text: Saint Francis of Assisi, 1182-1226, trans. © 1999 Franciscan Institute of St. Bonaventure University
Music: Joe Higginbotham, b.1953, © 2012 Joe Higginbotham

O, Our Father Most Holy

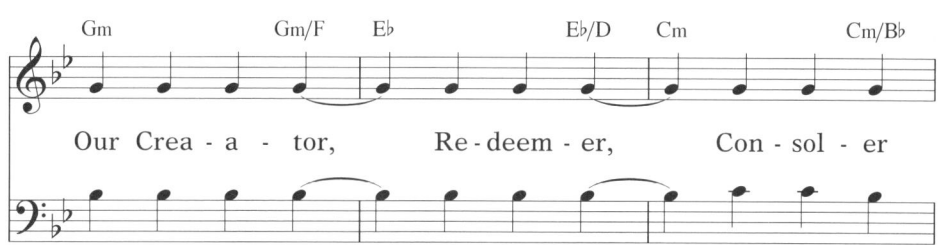

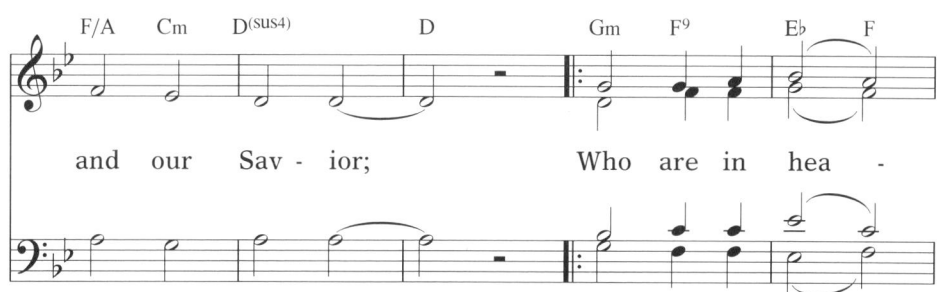

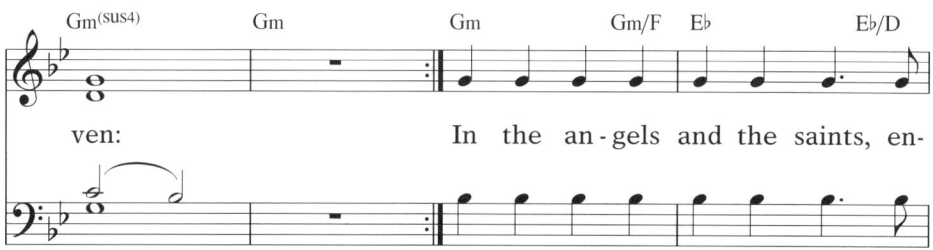

Text: Saint Francis of Assisi, 1182-1226, trans. © 1999 Franciscan Institute of St. Bonaventure University
Music: Joe Higginbotham, b.1953, © 2012 Joe Higginbotham

Text: Saint Francis of Assisi, 1182-1226, trans. © 1999 Franciscan Institute of St. Bonaventure University
Music: Joe Higginbotham, b.1953, © 2012 Joe Higginbotham

Hail, Our Lady

Text: Saint Francis of Assisi, 1182-1226, trans. © 1999 Franciscan Institute of St. Bonaventure University
Music: Based on ALMA REDEMPTORIS, Chant; adapted by Joe Higginbotham, b.1953, © 2012 Joe Higginbotham

Praises to Be Said at All the Hours

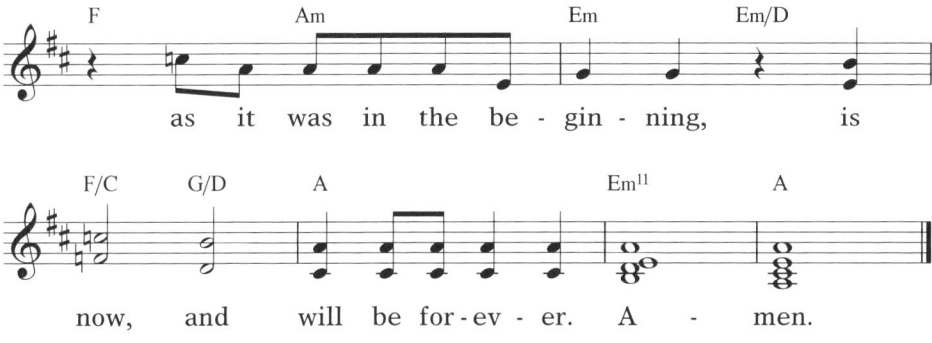

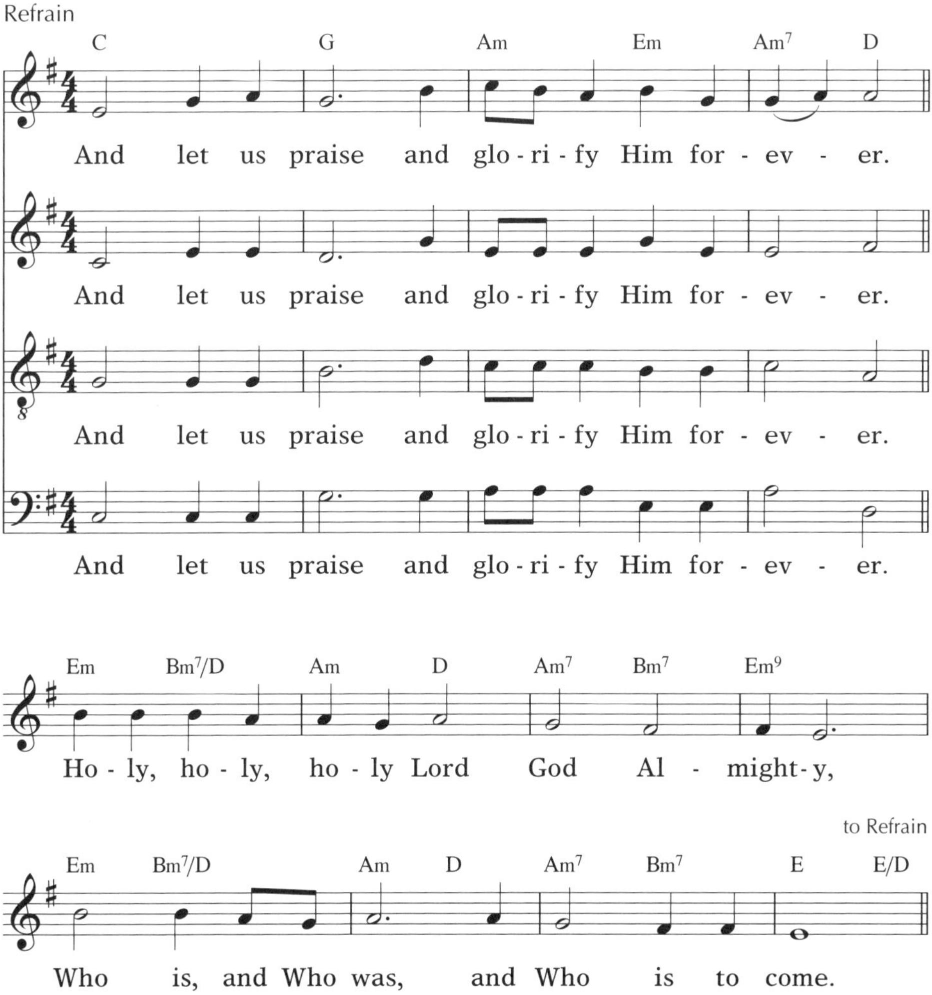

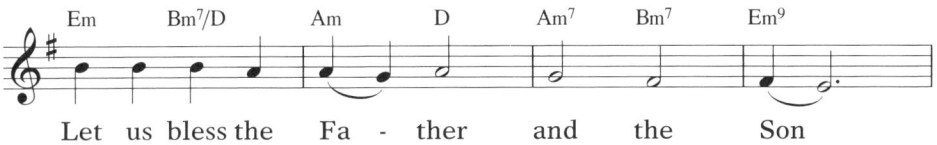
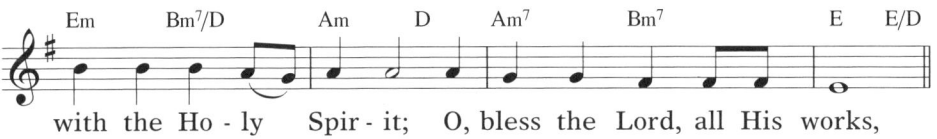

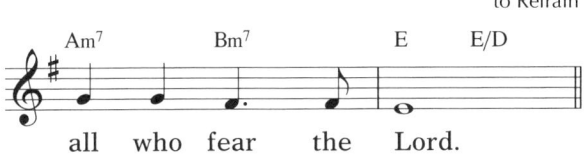
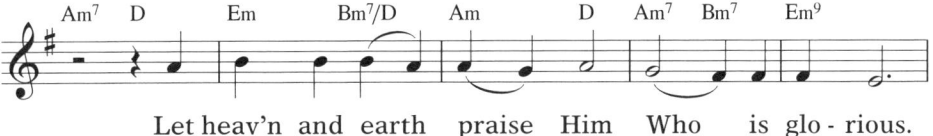

All-Powerful, Most Holy (a)

Text: Saint Francis of Assisi, 1182-1226, trans. © 1999 Franciscan Institute of St. Bonaventure University
Music: JESU DULCIS MEMORIA, Chant; adapted by Joe Higginbotham, b.1953, © 2012 Joe Higginbotham

All-Powerful, Most Holy (b)

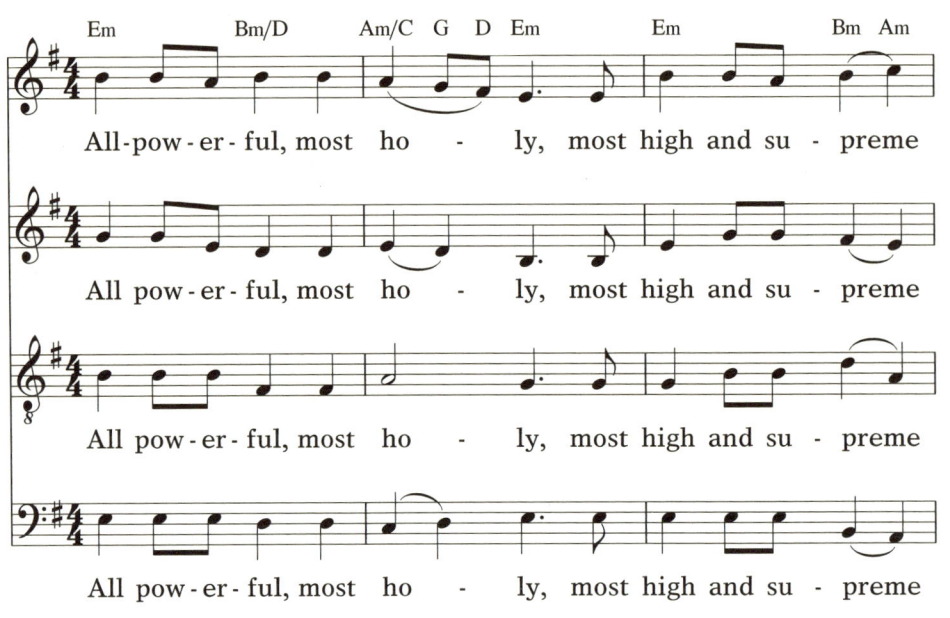
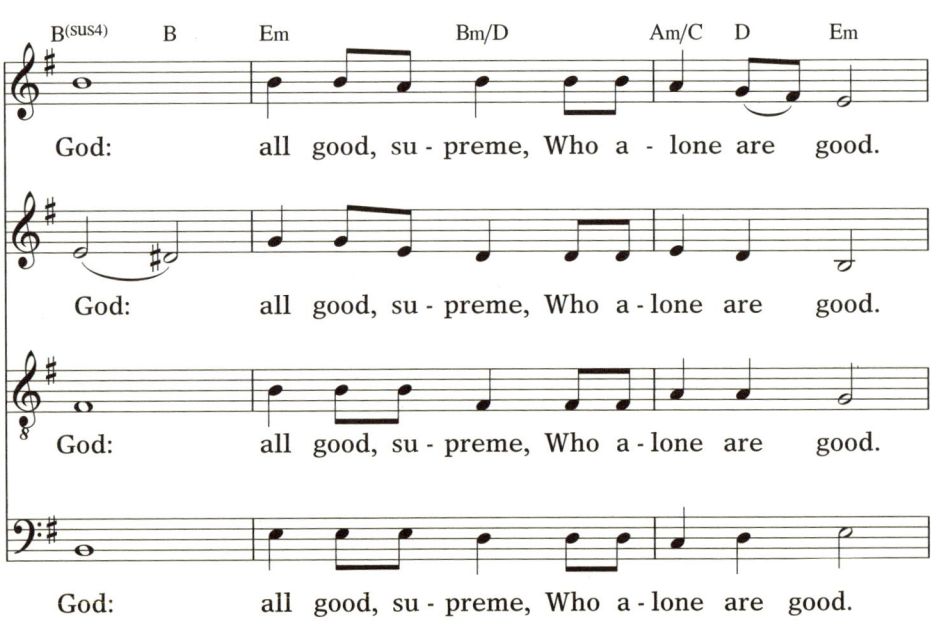

63

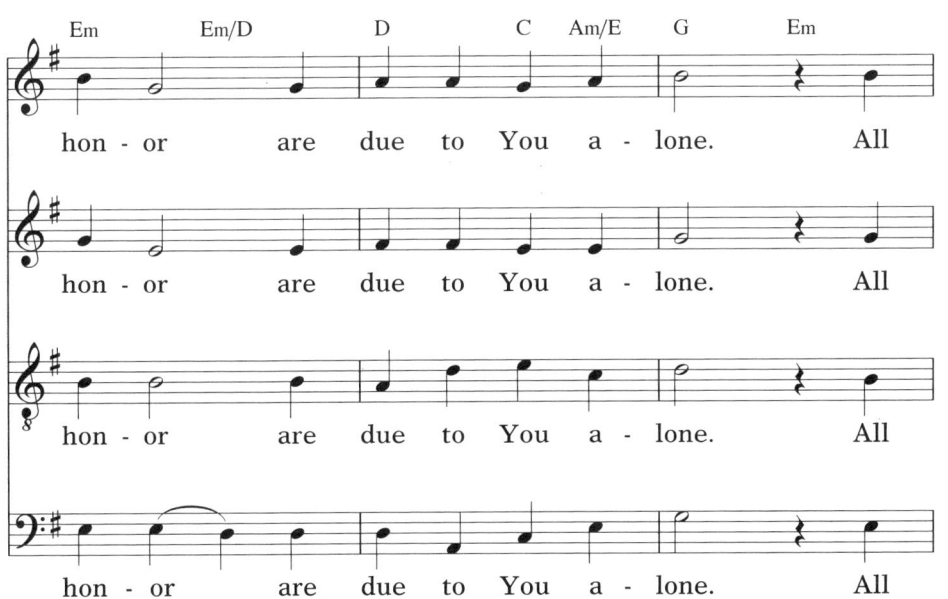

Text: Saint Francis of Assisi, 1182-1226, trans. © 1999 Franciscan Institute of St. Bonaventure University
Music: Joe Higginbotham, b.1953, © 2012 Joe Higginbotham

Holy Virgin Mary

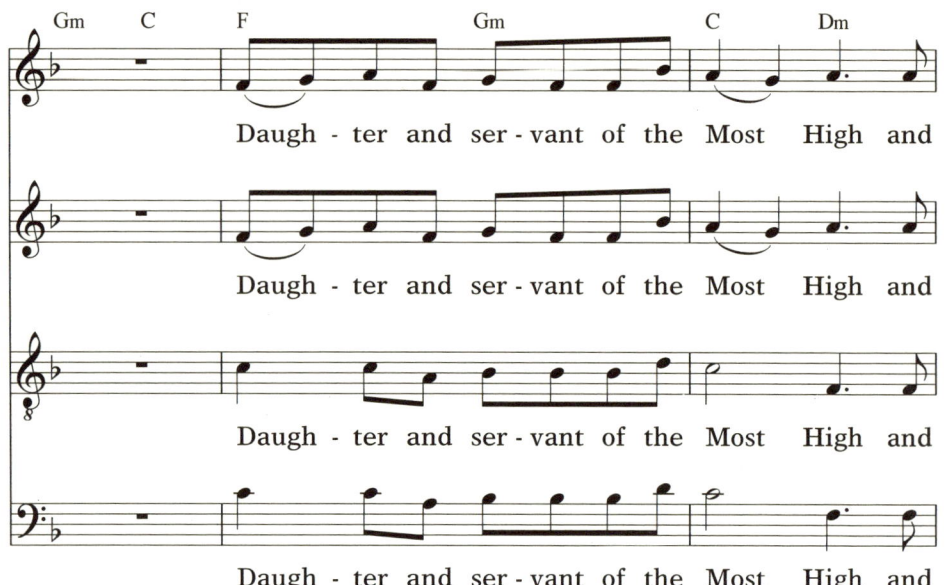
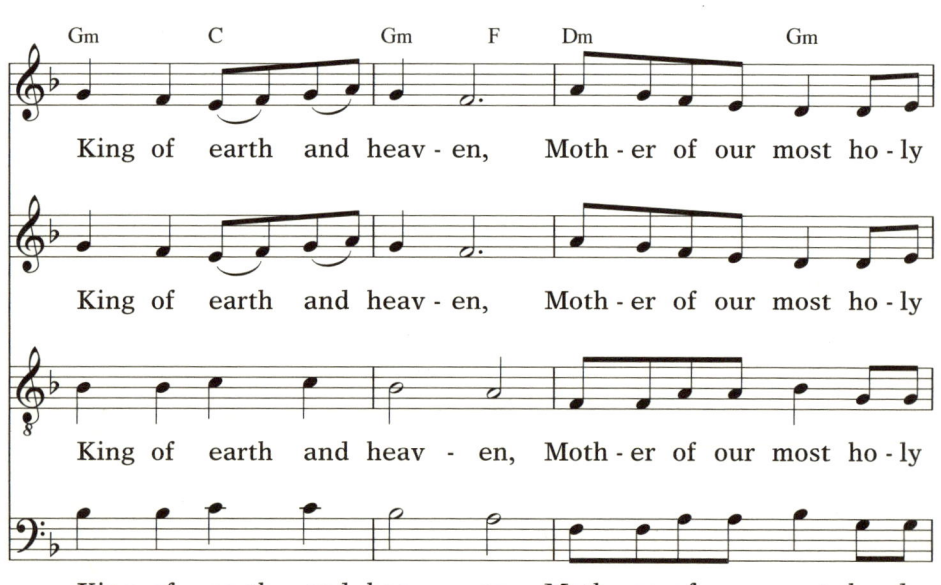

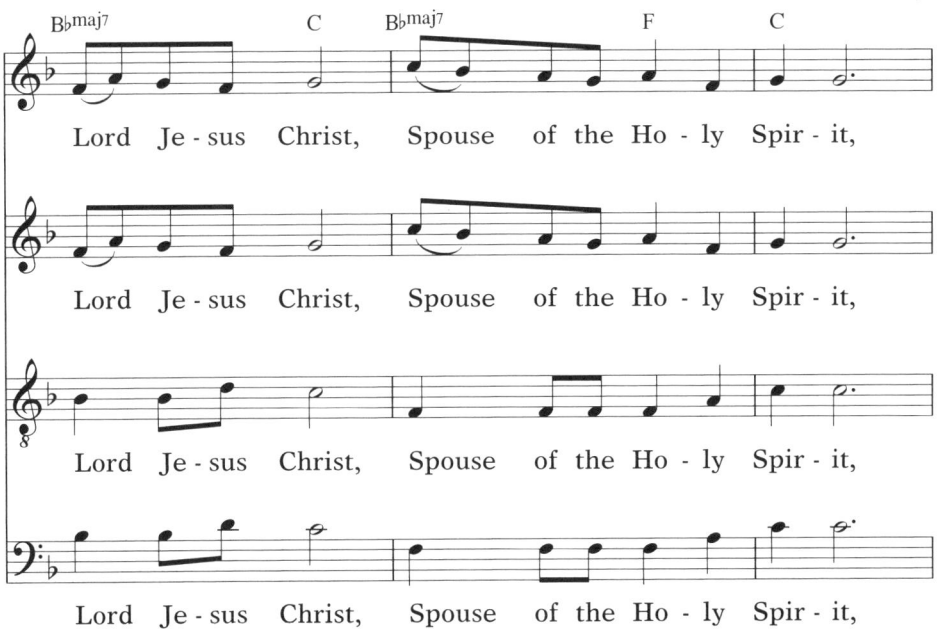

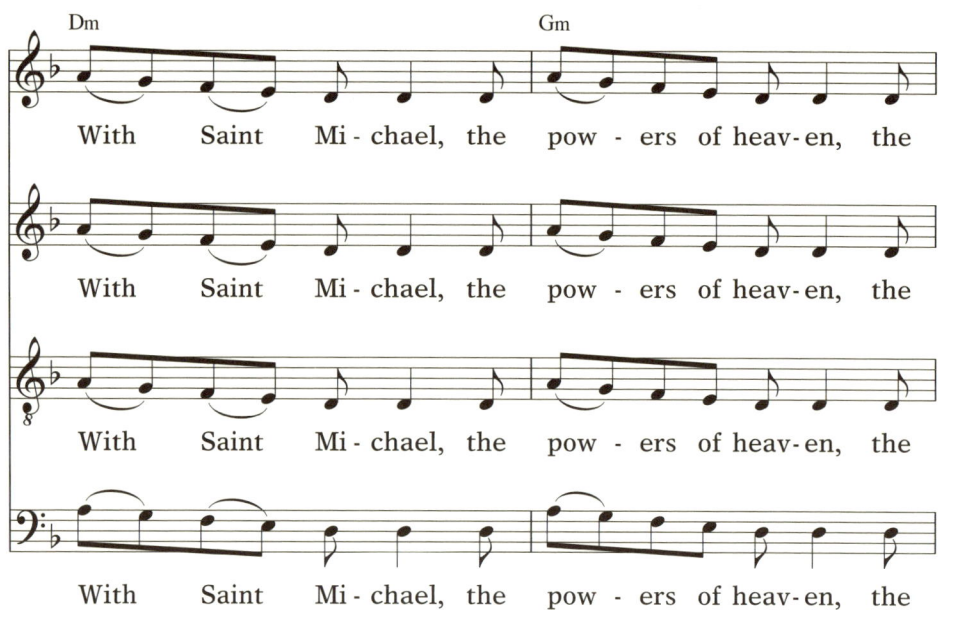
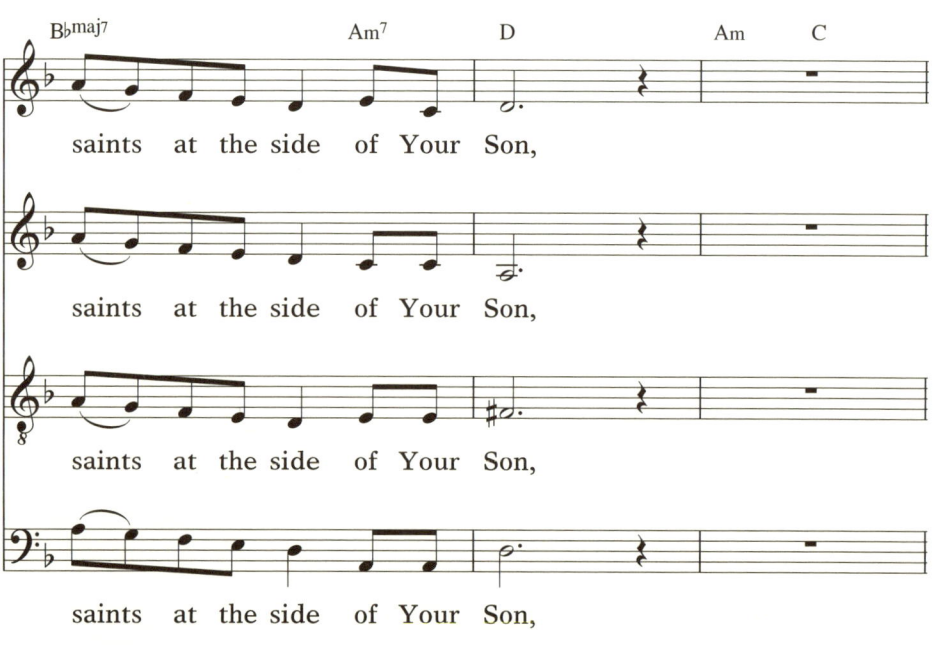

Psalm Tone 1

Psalm 1

God, I have told you of my life;
You have placed all my tears in your sight.
All my enemies were plotting against me;
they took counsel together.

They repaid me evil for good,
and hatred for my love.
They slandered me in return for my love,
but I continued to pray.

My holy Father, King of heaven and earth, / do not leave me
for trouble is near / and there is no one to help.
Let my enemies be turned back
on whatever day I shall call upon you; / for now I know that you are my God.

My friends and my neighbors have drawn near
and have stood against me;
those who were close to me
have stayed far away.

You have driven my acquaintances far from me;
they have made me an abomination to them.
I have been handed over
and did not escape.

Holy Father, do not remove your help from me,
my God, look to my aid.
Come to my help,
Lord, God of my salvation.

Glory to the Father, and to the Son,
and to the Holy Spirit:
As it was in the beginning, is now,
and will be forever. Amen.

Psalm Tone 6

Psalm 2

Lord, God of <u>my</u> salvation,
I cry day and night <u>to</u> you.
Let my prayer enter into <u>your</u> sight,
incline your ear <u>to</u> my prayer.

Attend to my <u>soul</u> and free it;
set me free because of <u>my</u> enemies.
For it was you who took me out of <u>the</u> womb,
you, my hope from my <u>mother</u>'s breasts.

I have been cast upon you <u>from</u> the womb.
From my mother's womb you have been <u>my</u> God.
Do not depart <u>from</u> me.
You know my disgrace, my confusion / <u>and</u> my reverence.

All those who trouble me are <u>in</u> your sight;
my heart has expected abuse <u>and</u> misery.
I looked for someone to grieve togeth<u>er</u> with me
and there was none, / for someone to console me / and <u>I</u> found none.

God, the wicked have ris<u>en</u> against me,
the assembly of the powerful has sought <u>my</u> life;
they have not placed you in <u>their</u> sight.
I am numbered among those who go down in<u>to</u> the pit,

I have become as someone without help, / cut off a<u>mong</u> the dead.
You are my most Holy Father, / my King and <u>my</u> God.
Come to <u>my</u> aid,
Lord God of <u>my</u> salvation.

Glory to the Father, and <u>to</u> the Son,
and to the Ho<u>ly</u> Spirit:
As it was in the beginning, <u>is</u> now,
and will be forev<u>er</u>. Amen.

Psalm Tone 3

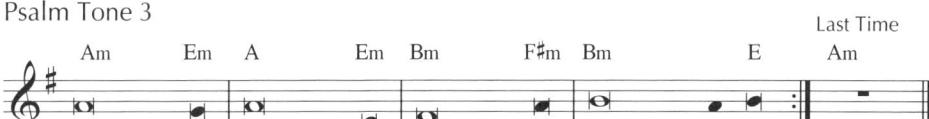

Psalm 3

Have mercy on me, O God, / have mercy on <u>me</u>
because my soul places its <u>trust</u> in you.
I will hope in the shadow of your <u>wings</u>
until wickedness <u>passes</u> by.

I will cry to the Most High God, / my most holy <u>Fa</u>ther,
who has done <u>good</u> to me.
He has sent from heaven and de<u>liv</u>ered me;
He has disgraced those who have trampled <u>up</u>on me.

God has sent His mercy and His <u>truth</u>;
He has snatched my life from the strongest of my <u>enemies</u>
and from those who hated me, / for they were too powerful for <u>me</u>.
They prepared a trap for my feet / and bowed down <u>my</u> soul.

They dug a pit before my <u>face</u>
and fell into it them<u>selves</u>!
My heart is ready, O God, / my heart is <u>rea</u>dy;
I will sing and chant <u>a</u> psalm.

Arise, my glory, / arise, psalter and <u>harp</u>,
I will arise at <u>dawn</u>,
I will praise you among the peoples, O <u>Lord</u>,
I will chant a psalm to you among <u>the</u> nations.

Because your mercy is exalted even to the <u>skies</u>,
and your truth even to the <u>clouds</u>.
be exalted above the heavens, O <u>God</u>,
and may your glory be over all <u>the</u> earth.

Glory to the Father, and to the <u>Son</u>,
and to the Holy <u>Spir</u>it:
As it was in the beginning, is <u>now,</u>
and will be forever. <u>A</u>men.

Psalm Tone 1

Psalm 4

Have mercy on me, O God, / for people have trampled me und<u>er</u>foot;
all day long they have afflicted me and fought <u>a</u>gainst me.
All day long my enemies trampled <u>up</u>on me
for there were many waging war <u>a</u>gainst me.

All my enemies have been thinking evil things <u>a</u>gainst me;
they made evil plots <u>a</u>gainst me.
Those who were guarding <u>my</u> life
have conspired t<u>o</u>gether.

They <u>went</u> out
and spread it ev<u>er</u>ywhere.
Seeing me, every<u>one</u> laughed at me;
they whispered and shook <u>their</u> heads.

I am a worm and <u>no</u> human,
the scorn of men and the outcast of <u>the</u> people.
I have been made despicable to <u>my</u> neighbors
far beyond all my enemies, / a thing of fear to all my <u>ac</u>quaintances.

O holy Father, do not keep your help <u>from</u> me,
but look to my <u>de</u>fense.
Come to <u>my</u> aid,
Lord, God of my s<u>al</u>vation.

Glory to the Father, and to <u>the</u> Son,
and to the Ho<u>ly</u> Spirit:
As it was in the beginning, <u>is</u> now
and will be forever. <u>A</u>men.

Psalm Tone 6

Psalm 5

I cried to the Lord with <u>all</u> my voice;
with all my voice I begged <u>the</u> Lord.
I pour out my prayer in <u>His</u> sight
and I tell the Lord of <u>all</u> my trouble.

When my <u>spi</u>rit failed me
you knew <u>my</u> ways.
On the path where <u>I</u> walked,
the proud hid a <u>trap</u> for me.

I looked to my <u>right</u> and saw;
there was no one <u>who</u> knew me.
I have no means of <u>es</u>cape;
there is no one who cares <u>for</u> my life.

I have borne abuse be<u>cause</u> of you
and confusion covers <u>my</u> face.
I have become an outcast to <u>my</u> brothers,
a stranger to the children <u>of</u> my mother.

Holy Father, zeal for your house <u>has</u> consumed me;
and the insults of those who blasphemed you / have fallen <u>on</u> me.
They rejoiced and united together <u>a</u>gainst me.
Blows were heaped on me and I <u>knew</u> not why.

More numerous than the hairs <u>of</u> my head
are those who hate me with<u>out</u> cause.
My enemies, who persecuted me unjustly, / have <u>been</u> strengthened;
I then repaid what I <u>did</u> not steal.

The wicked witnesses <u>who</u> rise up
asked me about things of which they <u>are</u> ignorant.
They repaid me evil for good and <u>ha</u>rassed me
be<u>cause</u> I pursued good.

You are my most <u>ho</u>ly Father,
my King and <u>my</u> God.
Come to <u>my</u> aid,
Lord, God of <u>my</u> salvation.

Glory to the Father, and <u>to</u> the Son,
and to the Ho<u>ly</u> Spirit:
As it was in the beginning, <u>is</u> now
and will be forev<u>er</u>. Amen.

Psalm Tone 6

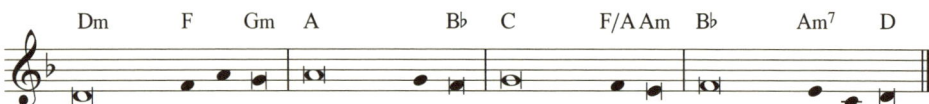

Psalm 6

O all you who pass a<u>long</u> the way,
look and see if there is any sorrow like <u>my</u> sorrow.
For many dogs surround<u>ed</u> me;
a pack of evildoers closed <u>in</u> on me.

They looked and <u>stared</u> at me;
they divided my garments <u>among</u> them
and they cast lots for <u>my</u> tunic.
They pierced my hands and my feet / they counted <u>all</u> my bones.

They opened their <u>mouths</u> against me,
like a raging and roar<u>ing</u> lion.
I have been poured out <u>like</u> water
and all my bones <u>have</u> been scattered.

My heart has become like <u>melt</u>ing wax
in the midst of <u>my</u> bosom.
My strength has been dried up like <u>baked</u> clay
and my tongue clings <u>to</u> my jaws.

They gave me gall <u>as</u> my food
And, in my thirst, / vinegar <u>to</u> drink.
They led me into the dust <u>of</u> death
and added sorrow <u>to</u> my wounds.

I have slept and risen
and my most holy Father has received me with glory.
Holy Father, / you held my right hand,
led me with your counsel / and have taken me up with glory.

For what is there in heaven for me,
and what do I want on earth besides you?
See, see that I am God, / says the Lord.
I shall be exalted among the nations / and exalted on the earth.

Blessed be the Lord,
the God of Israel,
Who has redeemed the souls of His servants
with His very own most holy Blood.

and Who will not abandon
all who hope in Him.
And we know that He is coming,
that He will come to judge justice.

Glory to the Father, and to the Son,
and to the Holy Spirit:
As it was in the beginning, is now
and will be forever. Amen.

Psalm Tone 4

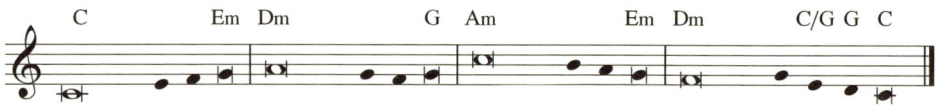

Psalm 7

All you nations, <u>clap</u> your hands,
shout to God with a <u>voice</u> of gladness.
For the Lord, <u>the</u> Most High,
the Awesome, / is the Great King o<u>ver</u> all the earth.

For the Most Holy Father of heaven, / our King be<u>fore</u> all ages
sent His beloved Son <u>from</u> on high
and has <u>brought</u> salvation
in the <u>midst</u> of the earth.

Let the heav<u>ens</u> rejoice
and the <u>earth</u> exult;
let the sea and all that is in <u>it</u> be moved;
let the fields and all that is <u>in</u> them be glad.

Sing a new <u>song</u> to Him.
Sing to the Lord, <u>all</u> the earth,
Because the Lord is great and highly <u>to</u> be praised,
awesome be<u>yond</u> all gods.

Give to the Lord, you fami<u>lies</u> of nations,
Give to the Lord glo<u>ry</u> and honor.
Give <u>to</u> the Lord
the glo<u>ry</u> due His name.

Take <u>up</u> your bodies
and carry His <u>holy</u> cross,
and follow His most ho<u>ly</u> commands
e<u>ven</u> to the end.

Let the whole earth tremble be<u>fore</u> His face;
tell among the nations that the Lord has ruled <u>from</u> a tree.
He ascended <u>into</u> heaven
and is seated at the right hand / of the most holy <u>Father</u> in heaven.

O God, be exalted a<u>bove</u> the heavens,
And above all the earth <u>be</u> your glory.
We know that <u>He</u> is coming,
that He will <u>come</u> to judge justice.

Glory to the Father, and <u>to</u> the Son,
and to the <u>Ho</u>ly Spirit:
As it was in <u>the</u> beginning,
is now and will be for<u>ev</u>er. Amen.

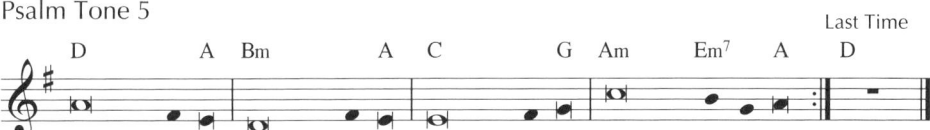

Psalm Tone 5

Psalm 8

O God, come to my <u>assistance</u>,
Lord, make haste <u>to</u> help me.
Let those who seek <u>my</u> life
be put to shame <u>and</u> confounded.

Let those who wish <u>me</u> evil
be put to flight and <u>disgraced</u>.
Let those who say to me: "Well done! / <u>Well</u> done!"
be turned <u>back</u> in shame.

May all those <u>who</u> seek you
exult and be glad <u>in</u> you
may those who love your salvation al<u>ways</u> say:
"May the <u>Lord</u> be glorified!"

But I am afflicted <u>and</u> poor;
help me, <u>O</u> God.
You are my help and my <u>de</u>liverer;
Lord, do <u>not</u> delay.

Glory to the Father, and to <u>the</u> Son,
and to the Ho<u>ly</u> Spirit:
As it was in the beginning, <u>is</u> now
and will be for<u>ev</u>er. Amen.

Psalm Tone 3

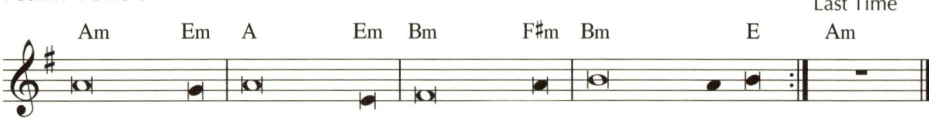

Psalm 9

Sing a new song to the <u>Lord,</u>
for He has done wonderful <u>things</u>.
His right hand and holy <u>arm</u>
have sacrificed His belov<u>ed</u> Son.

The Lord has made His salvation <u>known;</u>
has revealed his justice in the sight of the <u>nations</u>.
On that day the Lord has sent his <u>mercy,</u>
and at night <u>his</u> song.

This is the day the Lord has <u>made</u>;
let us rejoice and be <u>glad</u> in it.
Blessed is the one who comes in the name of the <u>Lord,</u>
the Lord is God, / and has enlight<u>ened</u> us.

Let the heavens re<u>joice</u>
and the earth ex<u>ult;</u>
let the sea and all that is in it be <u>moved;</u>
let the fields and all that is in them <u>be</u> glad.

Give to the Lord, you families of <u>nations,</u>
Give to the Lord glory and <u>honor</u>.
Give to the <u>Lord</u>
the glory due <u>His</u> name.

*(The following three verses
are added during the Easter season.)*

Sing to the Lord, kingdoms of the <u>earth,</u>
sing psalms to the <u>Lord</u>.
Sing psalms to God / who ascends above the heights of the <u>heavens</u>
to the rising of <u>the</u> sun.

Behold, / the Lord will give his voice the voice of <u>power;</u>
give glory to <u>God</u>!
His greatness is over <u>Israel;</u>
His power is in <u>the</u> skies.

God is marvelous in his ho̲ly ones.
The God of Israel himse̲lf
will give power and strength to his pe̲ople.
Blessed be̲ God!

Glory to the Father, and to the So̲n,
and to the Holy Spi̲rit:
As it was in the beginning, is no̲w
and will be forever. A̲men.

Psalm Tone 4

Psalm 10

Cry out with joy to the Lord, a̲ll the earth;
Chant a psalm to his name / give glory to̲ his praise.
Say to God: / "How awesome are your wo̲rks, O Lord.
Your enemies shall fawn upon you / in the great̲ness of your strength.

Let all the earth adore you and sing a psa̲lm to you;
let us chant a psalm to̲ your name."
Come, listen, and I will tell you, / all you wh̲o fear God,
how much he has do̲ne for my soul.

I cried with my mo̲uth to him,
and I have exulted wi̲th my tongue.
From his holy temple / he he̲ard my voice
and my cr̲y reached His ears.

Bless our Lo̲rd, you peoples,
make the voice of his pr̲aise be heard.
May all the tribes of the earth be ble̲ssed in him,
and all nations wi̲ll glorify him.

Blessed be the Lord, the Go̲d of Israel,
Who alone do̲es great wonders.
Blessed forever be the name o̲f his majesty,
and may all the earth be filled with his majesty. / So be i̲t. So be it.

Glory to the Father, and <u>to</u> the Son,
and to the <u>Ho</u>ly Spirit:
As it was in the begin<u>ning</u>, is now
and will be for<u>ev</u>er. Amen.

Psalm 11

May the Lord hear you on the day of <u>your</u> distress,
may the name of the God of Ja<u>cob</u> protect you.
From the sanctuary may He <u>send</u> you help,
and from Sion may <u>he</u> sustain you.

May he remember all your <u>sac</u>rifices
and may your burnt offer<u>ing</u> be fruitful.
May he grant your <u>heart's</u> desires,
and fulfill your <u>ev</u>ery plan.

We will rejoice in <u>your</u> salvation,
and be glorified in the name of the <u>Lord</u> our God.
May the Lord fulfill all <u>your</u> requests,
now I have known that the Lord has sent Jesus <u>Christ</u> His Son,

and He will judge the peo<u>ples</u> with justice.
The Lord has become the refuge <u>of</u> the poor,
their help in <u>times</u> of trial.
Let those who know <u>your</u> name trust you.

Blessed be the <u>Lord</u> my God,
Who has be<u>come</u> my stronghold
and refuge on the day of <u>my</u> distress.
My help, I will sing a <u>psalm</u> to you,

Because you, God, <u>are</u> my stronghold,
My <u>God</u>, my mercy!

Glory to the Father, and <u>to</u> the Son,
and to the <u>Ho</u>ly Spirit:
As it was in the beginn<u>ing</u>, is now
and will be forev<u>er</u>. Amen.

Psalm 12

In you, Lord, I <u>have</u> hoped,
let me not be put <u>to</u> shame
in your justice, free me <u>and</u> rescue me.
Incline your ear to <u>me</u> and save me.

God, be my protector and <u>my</u> stronghold,
that you <u>may</u> save me.
Because you are my <u>pa</u>tience, Lord,
Lord, my hope <u>from</u> my youth.

From the womb I have been strengthened <u>in</u> you;
from my mother's womb you are my <u>pro</u>tector,
my song will always be <u>to</u> you.
May my mouth be <u>filled</u> with praise,

that I may sing of <u>your</u> glory,
and all day long of <u>your</u> greatness.
Hear me, Lord, because your mercy <u>is</u> kind;
look upon me according to the greatness <u>of</u> your mercies.

Do not turn your face from <u>your</u> child;
because I am afflicted, quick<u>ly</u> hear me.
Blessed be the Lord <u>my</u> God,
Who has been my protector and refuge / on the day <u>of</u> distress.

O <u>my</u> helper,
I will chant a psalm <u>to</u> you,
because you, O God, are my <u>pro</u>tector,
My <u>God</u>, my mercy.

Glory to the Father, and to the Son,
and to the Holy Spirit:
As it was in the beginning, is now
and will be forever. Amen.

Psalm Tone 1

Psalm 13

How long, Lord, will you forget me forever?
How long will you turn your face from me?
How long will I place doubts in my soul,
sorrow in my heart day after day?

How long will my enemy exult over me?
Look upon me and hear me, Lord, my God.
Give light to my eyes that I may never sleep in death,
so that my enemy may never say: / I have overcome him!

Those who afflict me would rejoice if I stumble / but I have hoped in your
    mercy.
My heart shall rejoice in your salvation;
I will sing to the Lord Who gives me good things.
I will chant a psalm / to the name of the Lord the Most High.

Glory to the Father, and to the Son,
and to the Holy Spirit:
As it was in the beginning, is now
and will be forever. Amen.

Psalm Tone 4

Psalm 14

I will praise you, Lord, Most Holy Father, / King of heav<u>en</u> and earth,
because you <u>have</u> consoled me.
You are <u>God</u>, my Savior,
I will act with confidence and <u>not</u> be afraid.

The Lord is my strength <u>and</u> my glory,
He has become <u>my</u> salvation.
Your right hand, Lord, / has been glori<u>fied</u> in strength;
your right hand, Lord, / <u>has</u> struck my enemy.

In the greatness <u>of</u> your glory
you have de<u>posed</u> my adversaries.
May the poor see <u>and</u> rejoice,
seek God and <u>your</u> soul shall live.

Let heaven <u>and</u> earth praise Him,
the sea and every living <u>thing</u> in them.
Because God <u>will</u> save Sion,
the cities of Judah <u>will</u> be rebuilt.

They <u>will</u> dwell there
and acquire it <u>by</u> inheritance.
The descendants of God's servants <u>will</u> possess it,
and those who love <u>God's</u> name will dwell there.

Glory to the Father, and <u>to</u> the Son,
and to the <u>Holy</u> Spirit:
As it was in the begin<u>ning</u>, is now
and will be for<u>ev</u>er. Amen.

Psalm Tone 2   Last Time

Psalm 15

Exult in <u>God</u> our help!
Shout to the Lord God, living and true, / with <u>cries</u> of gladness,
because the Lord, <u>the</u> Most High,
the Awesome, / is the Great King over <u>all</u> the earth,

because the Most Holy Father of heaven, / our King be<u>fore</u> all ages,
sent His Beloved Son <u>from</u> on high
and He was born of the Blessed Virgin <u>Ho</u>ly Mary.
He called to me: / You <u>are</u> my Father

and I will place Him, my firstborn, <u>as</u> the Highest,
above all the kings <u>of</u> the earth.
On that day the Lord <u>sent</u> His mercy,
and at <u>night</u> His song.

This is the day the <u>Lord</u> has made;
let us rejoice and be <u>glad</u> in it.
For the Most Holy Child has been <u>given</u> to us
and has been born for us <u>on</u> the way

and placed <u>in</u> a manger
because he did not have a place <u>in</u> the inn.
Glory to the Lord God <u>in</u> the highest,
and peace on earth to those <u>of</u> good will.

Let the heavens rejoice and the <u>earth</u> exult,
let the sea <u>and</u> its fullness resound,
let the fields and all that is in <u>them</u> be joyful.
Sing a new song <u>to</u> the Lord,

sing to the Lord <u>all</u> the earth.
Because the Lord is <u>great</u> and worthy of praise
He is awesome be<u>yond</u> all gods.
Give to the Lord, you fami<u>lies</u> of nations,

give to the Lord gl_o_ry and praise,
give to the Lord the glory d_ue_ His name.
Take up your bodies and carry His h_o_ly cross
And follow His most holy commands even t_o_ the end.

Glory to the Father, and t_o_ the Son,
and to the H_o_ly Spirit:
As it was in the beginn_ing_, is now
and will be for_e_ver. Amen.

Holy Virgin Mary
(pg. 65)

Blessing – Dismissal (a)

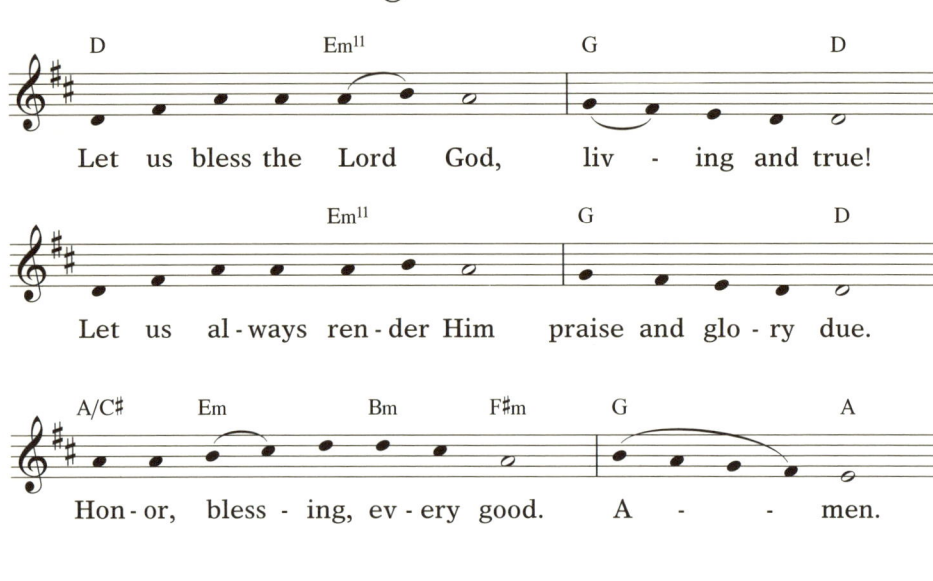

Text: Saint Francis of Assisi, 1182-1226, trans. © 1999 Franciscan Institute of St. Bonaventure University
Music: ADORO TE DEVOTE, Chant; adapted by Joe Higginbotham, b.1953, © 2012 Joe Higginbotham

Blessing – Dismissal (b)

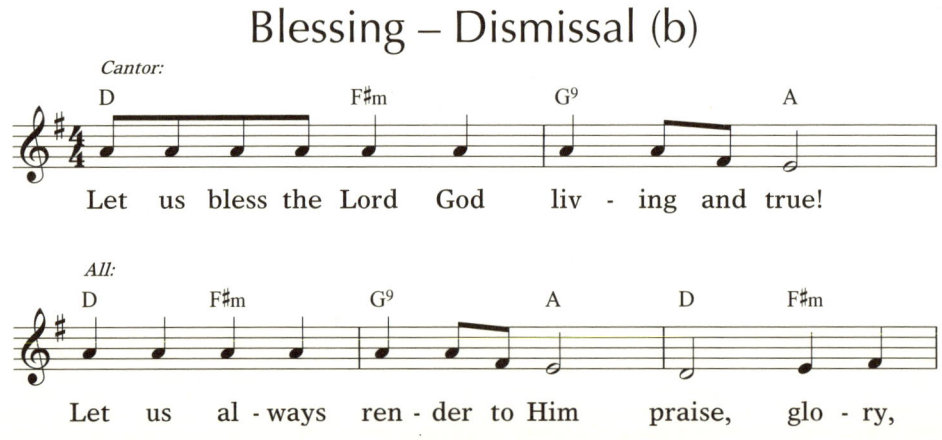

89

End of Office of the Passion

Text: Saint Francis of Assisi, 1182-1226, trans. © 1999 Franciscan Institute of St. Bonaventure University
Music: Joe Higginbotham, b.1953, © 2012 Joe Higginbotham

Prayer Of Saint Francis

1. Lord, make me an in-stru-ment of Your bless-ed peace.
2. Where there is great de-spair, hope in You must reign.
3. O Di-vine Mas-ter, grant that I not seek
4. It is in our giv-ing that we do re-ceive.

Where there is ha-tred, let Your love in-crease.
Where there is dark-ness, bring Your light a-gain.
con-so-la-tion, but a heart hum-ble, pure, and meek.
It is in our par-don-ing that we are set free.

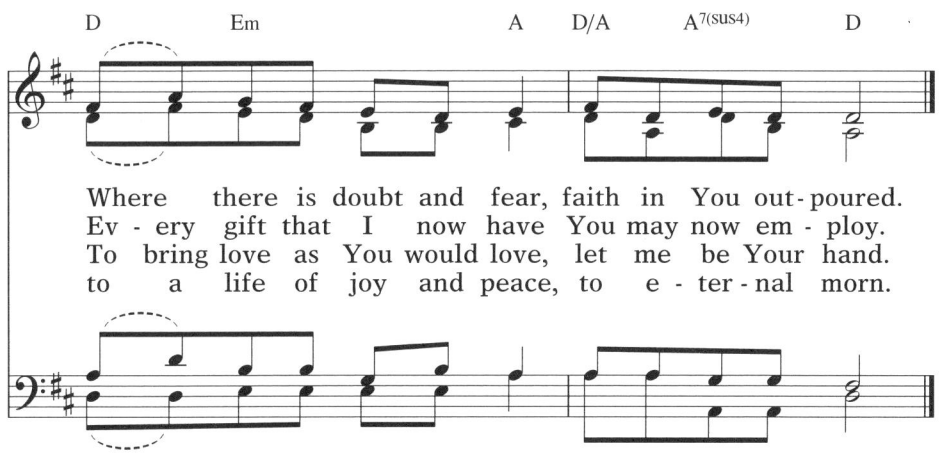

Text: Saint Francis of Assisi, 1182-1226, trans. © 1999 Franciscan Institute of St. Bonaventure University
Music: ADORO TE DEVOTE, Chant; adapted by Joe Higginbotham, b.1953, © 2012 Joe Higginbotham